THE BOOK OF
ELEGIAC GEOGRAPHY

poems by

Sam Hamill

BOOKSTORE PRESS

Thanks to the editors of the following publications where some of these poems first appeared: *dalmo'ma*, *Iron Rock Press*, *Jawbone*, *Silver Vain*, *Portland Review*, *Montana Gothic*, *Raindance*, *Yakima*, *Vegetable Box*, *Cutbank*, and *Kuksu*. Special thanks to Sam Green at Jawbone Press for permission to reprint several poems from the chapbook *Living Light*. "First Psalm" was issued as a pamphlet, hors commerce, from Copper Canyon Press.

ISBN 0-912846-29-1 cloth
ISBN 0-912846-30-5 paper

BOOKSTORE PRESS
Box 191, RFD #1
Freeport, Maine 04032

CONTENTS

for Eron

"Culture's outlived, art's rootcut, discovery's
The way to walk in. Only remains to invent the language
  to tell it. Match-ends of burnt experience
Human enough to be understood,
Scraps and metaphors will serve." —Robinson Jeffers

"I hope to become a rock." —Edward Abbey

Alyeska

FOR WAGES

Late night black coffee
from beans ground by hand

endless cigarettes silence
in snowy pine

two thousand miles from home

LETTER FROM ANCHORAGE

In alleys off Fourth Avenue
sad natives drink tokay, *Thunderbird*
to obliterate the day.
Bookstore windows say *Adult*
in home-made signs. The sky's
a careless smudge of soot
on this gray day and promises
no more warmth than mud.
Trees are painted garish
as any pipeline whore,
and every door on every block
repeats a condemnation
in the language of a lock.

But down the road
the air is crisply clear:
no shiny shoes out there.
Out there, that's called *debris*.
Light frost last week
and again today predicts
the lessening of light,
and leaves from every tree in sight remark
the chill autumnal breeze.

Moist tundra north of here
is hunting ground—
fishing out of there,
shooting moose, bear, and in winter
caribou. In villages on native lands
the Eskimos stay dry. Sick drunks
ride boats down stream four hours
to drink in Dillingham.

And back downtown, there's wolves
and snarling bears
in every storefront glass,
the souvenirs imported
from Seattle, Arizona, or Taiwan.
In Bootlegger Cove, the sailboats gone,
the water's muddy pale. Another year,
the summer gone. Another year, no whales.

X:76

A SNAPSHOT OF PORTAGE GLACIER

Raw to the wind
and naked as desire, I stand
in dying light, October,
dazzled at her feet.
Pale, she stretches,
rolling between the peaks,
also naked, unashamed,
a Paleolithic glow
beneath the surface of her skin.

ALYESKA, KAIPAROWITS, & BEYOND

Night. The last streetlight
spins off into starry heavens.
A freezing dark limps 'round the house
and down the tidy block
toward icy blue Alaskas
where a salmon-colored sun
sinks low
in cold October ashes.

Along the cove, old tracks
wither into rust
despite the trains at 8 a.m.
and afternoons at five.
No roads left
but ribbons of blue beyond
the shriveling pumpkins
and potatoes hard as stones
inside their shell of soil.
Hoarfrost glazes marshes
where late herons sail low
through bare aspen
glistening in the dark.

Outside Portage, the glacier calves
across the gray, implacable water.
My breath hangs before me
naked cold
as mist above a river. The brittle air
rises up inside my eyes. The moon,
that alabaster moon,
pours down at night
like ivory thighs when stars

dance off through indifferent skies
like adolescent girls. Mountains
heaped like cairns
hang white above the tideflats
dark with magic silt.

Twenty years ago
I dug the long pitchfork tongs
into heavy crust in a chicken coop,
ammonia blearing my eyes
and rifling through my lungs
with each deep stab into dung.
The quonset shed brimmed with hay
to feed a renegade mare. Chocked bins
bulged with grain
and Utah winds alternately bruised and buoyed
the snow-dappled Oquirrh Range.
I listened at night
for the low moans of coal trains
until a plume of whiskey-colored dawn
poured honey through the trees.

Now two thousand miles north,
the tracks run to their end,
nothing left
but the frozen sea
and great baleens—giant blues
curling with their calves
above or through the reefs.

When that pickup hit the grizzly,
forty miles away,

it hauled its thousand pounds
a hundred yards down the highway
and into screaming traffic.
Hit twice again, it sprawled
in alder saplings by the road
and took three ten-gauge slugs,
massive shaggy head lolled sideways,
eyes rolling
in the skull, pumping blood
and frosty breath
for an agonizing hour.

Across the northern tundra,
aluminum arteries pump up black blood
from the fleshy meat of this world.
And in the sandstone wilderness of Zion,
the Kaiparowits Project failed.
Ah, weep
for the savage luxuries of men
whose cruelties go unnamed.
Last caribou
munch brown winter tundra grass,
their migratory trails destroyed.
Their large eyes slowly burn
with the intelligence of fear.
What's dear
is always dearest when it's gone.
A life is a history of goodbyes.

FIRE AND ICE IN WINTER

Dear Tree,
Shivering in rain that plummets
through frozen spidery streets
saddled with snow from a month ago,
my boots dissolving
on the winter-salted avenue,
the glittering cold
of half a life of solitude
fogging the latitudes of vision,

I remember the sheen of your hair
in the firelight how many years ago
in warm coast winds
thousands of miles south of here—
we had no furniture and lived
on the rough wood floor
of a ramshackle crack in the hill.

And years later, in a bar
like a bad joke in Denver,
bewildered by a fever
no medicine could cure,
I called you with a renovating plan.
(Lord, the shots I poured
to meet the price
a mortgaged tongue demands.)
Somewhere down one of a hundred roads
it seems that plan fell finally down.

I remember the taste of dirt,
vertigo and neon,
empty alleyways at 3 a.m.

when even drunks go home. I went home
to a different home each night.

A faint sun slants across white ice
in gray salt water beside
the railroad ties I trudge. It is,
I think, a kind of wound
that stirs the sleeping fever,
Kafka's rose
that blossoms in our brains and grows
until only spikey thorns remain
to bleed us of all pain
when we are fearful and alone.

I remember your earth-colored hair
and a thousand winter fires
dying in your eyes.
Mercenary clouds explode
more rain against
the glowering Kenai Range. Lightning
rivers from the sky.
A man can burn or harden into ice.

Over the frozen earth,
I tramp home again
to another home
to think of you
and of what in the world
is good.

It is winter. I am cold,
though not alone.
And I can send you nothing
but what I am without,
and that is what I send.

I:77

THEOSOPHY & GEOLOGY IN THE FLESH

A great, golden bird
soars on brilliant wings
between twin icy peaks
in the Chugach Range.

And last night, in my sleep,
in my dreams, you rose
like a soft warm star,
your skin barely visible
beneath a gauze chemise,
your brown hair smelling rich
as river valley topsoil.

Unseasonable warm weather,
ice breaking up in the water,
and old ravens peruse
the transparent pages of heaven.
Fireweed sleeps
across ten thousand fields,
awaiting the fires of spring.

And here, the world ends,
crumbles away in snowy chunks
drifting out across the sea.
And the moribund souls of a nation
of avaricious men grow small,
futilely wan,
in the cold hard light
of tenacious northern dawns.

A SNAPSHOT OF SUSITNA

Rising in a creamy glow
through blue-black night
beneath the eyes of stars,
her feline curves
classic and mature,
she shifts, she sighs;
gentle,
white-skinned lovely
under silken sheets
of winter snow she sleeps
with the odd, peaceful smile
of eternal satisfaction
as attends the lips
of an ageless lover
when the full moon drifts
across the rim of the sky.

LETTER TO NANCY STEELE

High above the low, smoky-blue
February clouds, a single-prop plane
whines through the afternoon
toward another falling sun.
The city streets, wet with rain
and soft half-melted ice, teem
with weekend traffic. Paradise
is Celsius one degree.

I'm told the ravens here
live ninety years or more.
Unashamed, they congregate
to feast on refuse in the street,
strutting through gutters
beside booted, scurrying feet,
twisting their scuffled necks
to cock one angry eye
at any sign of intrusion
from any passerby.

They long outlast the fireweed
blazing in the hills,
the handsome magpies with delicate tails
gliding low across
a thousand summer fields. They survive
on terror and legend and shout
with a cracking voice,
saving their finest songs
for the music of their wings.

Stunted Sitka spruce grow dense
beyond the edge of town. Their limbs

are green, no sign of snow, their trunks
more slender than a thigh. A grove
of birch thrusts ominous
black and spidery boughs
from trunks as pale as cream.
In the moonlight of a clear cold night
they ring like the ghost of a chime.

Standing in the roadside shadow,
half lost in shadows of trees,
bewildered or amused, an old cow moose
nibbles her winter grass
watching traffic rush for Eagle River
or for Chugiak. Her great ears
turn at a horn or at
a diesel stack. Her wide nostrils flare
with every passing breath.

The last rays of daylight
limp across the peaks. Another plane
dies into night with a shriek.
I remember the insane flat roads
of Iowa, the legends that went sour.
I remember the heat of the south,
the bright autumn-in-Montana tamarack.
The nights fall thick about me,
cold as a raven's wing. The rented sheets
are cool across my back. I sleep
to dream unsettling dreams, hoping
all these aching, aging bones can make
the next town, somehow, home.

THE LOST FRONTIER

1. *Anchorage On Out*

"I first saw this land
on a mule. Been here
since nineteen and twelve."

Her dark
raisin-wrinkled eyes
peered out the big glass door
where lawyers walked the street.

"I wintered on Denali
and damned near froze to death."

Her coffee cup
rattled in her hand.

"Just look out there.
God damn.
Architects from L.A."

Huge square boxes,
flat-roofed
with glassed-in walls.

"Californicators, done that, boy.
Drove me out. And now
I'm goin back to Skagway."

2. *Ketchikan Rain*

Walked the beach
outside of town,
waiting for a plane:

shells and barnacles
ground to sand
under D8 tracks;
sulphur pulp-mill smoke
rising high;
log-trucks grumbling
round a curve—

turned back toward town
where boats drift by
with salmon iced-down
and piled high;
gift shops full
of Tlingit imitations
(like Yellowstone spring)

and the ticket counter
clerk says, "Gee,
goin Outside, huhm?
Must be nice
going back
to real civilization."

Deseret

THE BEAUTY OF PENANCE IN DESERET

Tonight I sprawl in a nine-dollar motel
in Nephi, Utah, gaping into the darkness
falling out my window, listening to diesels
charge the jack-pined hills beyond
the southwest end of town. Along the road
thin beeves parade in technicolor dust.
A renegade wind must carve
the high stone catacombs brown hawks
glide slowly down from. Across the hills
the twilight glints in picture postcard red
or what Alaskans call the eyelashes of the sun,
as though through a thousand copper clouds
a few lean rays escape to roam
vermillion sandstone canyons.

Two hours later, eight oh eight,
a train plunges through on its whistle.
Paralyzed, still contrite at the window,
I imagine a bone-wracked sandy plain
strewn far and wide with dread: it serves,
though feebly, as a conscience for a man.
The enigmatic night curls softly into frost.
Although by any estimate it isn't much,
I'm good at being what I am: half lost,
half found, guilty of excessive wine
and lust. Far off, a carnal wind explores
the skirts of a clapboard country house.
Dreams are things so lean in Deseret
that men abandon hopes all dreams protect.

AT THE RAILHEAD, GREYBULL WYOMING

Norwester winds out the window
play in the high plains sand
making winter desert flowers
like the iron filing rose
the magnet always forms. Worn ponies
graze with their rumps to that wind
across a hundred ranches
driving north from Thermopolis.
Between the distant Tetons
and the blue gray Bighorn peaks
an hour east of Lovell,
clouds drift through in herds
as formidable, as endless as our fathers
thought the herds of bison were.
Half dozen cows across the ancient tracks
stir up a little dust plodding doggedly
down a sage-lined trail south.
Two old cowboys creased deep
as the Wind River Range mutter
over coffee at the counter,
Stetsons set back and sweat-stained,
old boots worn down by the acids
found in dung. Outside in the wind,
a hinge on a boxcar door complains.

STILL LIFE IN PARAGONAH

for Dave and Jan

The year moves up the bluff and over
until only its long shadow remains
among the shadows of mesquite
and jack-pine and coarse Utah sage.
A light snow salted the higher hills
where magnificent icicles reflect
burnt-orange blazing canyon walls.
Deer at twilight graze beside the highway.
Leathery desert rabbits hypnotized
by diesel lights perish nightly
under truckers' wheels. A trained eye
roaming the hillocks in dying light
still finds a scrappy coyote
trotting warily through the shrub.

A pale finger of smoke points up
from the farmhouse chimney as though
it were raised in contention. It points
to the tough old stars which were born
and which die in the cool night
to the percussive symphony of crickets
mating in new-mown fields, grunts
and bellyaches of happiness floating
from the sty. Listen. Slow swish,
in the dark, of a horsetail.
And huddled round a fire men discuss
what they think are their problems
under the wisdom of heavens
in the star-crossed desert night.

TALKING GARY SNYDER
LONE TREE FARM POEM

Blue Uintah sky, no snow,
no skiers; magpies curl high over
over-grazed pastures, mid-air—
making love.

Rising early, cool frosty ground
crunches under heel. Our fathers thought
the beaver and bison inexhaustible.

Lay around all day, stay
loose, dreamy; still
doing things the old (and best) way: cook
turkey soup on the woodstove,
cornmeal muffins and thick
honey-sweet peach pie.

Watching the sun go down:
green gray phlegm
coughed up
from the throat of the valley.
This living quivering world
a single
breathing organism,
and we, we
live inside and on it,
germ-like—
what
and who
we are.

Envoi

Low rolling Uintah Peaks
drift off, feminine,
sun on warm December
asphalt road the long-legged
woman strides down.

Starlings curl high
on invisible waves.

"The stonework under the house,"
Pat says,
"is a hundred years old.
Easy to find. The only
tree in the valley."

Yes,
and the roots,
the dark roots
grip deep
and hold.

SANCTUARY

for Barbara

I.

Dry grass, dry clumps of sagebrush
on hills of clay and sandstone,
the streambeds shrivelled,
lakes gone to mud—Park City,
and scabby sheared sheep
graze the hills, blue heelers
and border collies
nipping their heels
as they strip the crusty land.

"Aint but one thang
dumber'n a god damn sheep."

"Whassat?"

"God damn sheep man."

II.

Afternoon fists of wind
flail cottonwoods and aspen stands
surrounding the narrow canyon town.
Above, from rising summits,
wide bulldozed skiing swaths
ride plunging naked crests.
Below, a faded white picket fence
frames old-fashioned upright tombstones
bleaching like bones in the sun.

Thousands and thousands
of years tell their lives
in sediment and striations
that endure the silly progress
and half-conscious pastimes
of undemocratic men.

While city fathers
debate the myriad human uses
of the world's last drop of water,
I suffer a thirst that only
Olympic rain can quench:
the womanly damp ground, easy to love,
the love of a woman called Tree, and,
the natural holy and tender anarchy
of the land.

MAN IN THE LANDSCAPE

I.
Thirty years since I walked
the slow fields of winter,
red-brown snow of Uintah
photographed in sepia,
fence-barbs tipped with frost,
moved among Depression-era faces
mauled by half a century
of working in the weather,

and saw then my first coyote,
an old licorice root
chewed to pieces, a
skinny bit of a thing,
hind leg wired to a fence post,
jaws wired shut,
still half alive and quivering,

and I heard Old Man Packer
(some said he was Albert's brother)
sawed the jaw from another
and set it loose for his dogs
and laced packets of pigfat with strychnine
and scattered them in the hills,

and my mother's mother
slept beside her bedpan,
the small bones of each breath
rattling in the linen,
and my father wanted
to explain it all away
but he couldn't,

and in that old brick house
built by my father and mother
important things went unsaid,
I learned to mourn silent early
and wear a cerement of sweat.

II.

"Nowadays they use ten-eighty,"
the government trapper said.
"Kills a damned sight more'n coyotes.
Put me out a work."

We walked a low knoll
and down a wide sandy path
through patches of chewed grass,
clusters of sage and thistle,
down to the riverbank
to gaze at broad cracks in the mud.

"Found a hawk.
Up there a ways," he said,
and peered into his hands.
"Dead. And a marten once,
but that was a while back."
He bit a nip from his plug,
chewed, and spit.

Then raised his eyes
to the sky. "Mice,
jackrabbits, magpies.
I seen antelope hittin' fences
at fifty miles an hour.
And that aint a pretty thing to see.

This here's sheep country, boy.
Sheep man is king. My traps
hang on my cabin wall. Shit,
it's gettin' so's any more
a man's got nowheres to go,
he wants to die alone."

III.
Ten-eighty spread on high plains,
TCDD spread all through the forests
where Smohalla asked,
"Would you tear the flesh
from your mother?
Cut her delicate long hair?"

Today a small brown sparrow
crashed into my window
and fell with a broken neck.
It died in the palm of my hand.
I set aside my shovel
and walked the D8 tracks
across a clear-cut slope
where I stopped at a stump
for a smoke.

A blackberry tangle
lay ripped and broken, vines
peeled back, stalks ragged
where metal treads eat land.
Vine maple, waxy green salal
already reclaim the soil.

Half-ripe berries survived
on tattered vines. Two finches
darted overhead, playing in the air.
The sign read *Private Property*
and I thought, *My god,*
she's still alive.

IV.
I waken early.
A light wind tips bare branches
with frost. Out my window,
the Cascades glow pink with dawn.
To the west, a dark Olympic blue.

A small plane passes over,
low. All over America,
men begin their work,
poisoning earth and air—
ten eighty, *TCDD*.

Soon, there'll be nothing left
but man,
alone in a poison landscape
learning the cold geography
of elegies.

Far off, Coyote yips and barks,
and slowly, another day begins.

Ish Province

INTERLUDE
in memoriam, Jackie Wheeler

blue
rising out of the blue sea in waves,
breaking over the stony shore,
seafoam, brine, soft breath
of the seawinds, wet sand,
the faraway gull on the wing,
thistled cliff rising high
above drifting wave and loam,
the great blue heron dipping its wings
into the rolling wave-peaks, dark shadow
wobbling the water below,
head tucked back for flight,
large wide feet tucked up behind
as he glides,

and the sun a shadowy orange,
dark orange the horizon,
and the blue blue sky swimming up
through a few thin clouds to the north,
and islands rising in the tide,
timbered, rock-shored, lifting
from blue sea to sea-blue sky,
green overflowing, and the whistle
of a boat out of sight, borne up
on the easy wave, the men and women on deck
with their backs sloping back on the nets,

and the white shells on the shore
turn blue in the evening light,
first pink and then blue
in the dying evening light

that calls up the depths of the sea
where rock-crabs dawdle sideways in the sand
and sandworms drowse at the shore
and razor clams sift the water
in their secret boney homes,
and the horseclams palaver
in the sea's secret chambers
and the sandcrabs imitate their elders . . .

ah, and Ezra's Kung
talks of "grasping the azure . . . "
to comprehend the blue of the sky,
the seaward rowing fishes,
and on *Dawntreader*'s deck
we gazed out across the water,
dark blue of the riptides,
pale blue to green in the shallows,
and the small jib billowed on the bow,
and the fores'l unfurled
in handcrafted heavenly white,
the puffins bobbed and dove
as the breezes sang through the rigging . . .

and Thetis, sea-goddess whose watery hand
set tide to ebb or flood
invented the dance of fertility
in islands not far from these, green hills,
green shores at the distant edge
of a thousand distant seas . . .

and in the evening light,
the nighthawks jibber and dive,

their frantic erratic flight
hurling them down with a flutter . . .
the estuaries shimmer in the shallows
where soft rivers drown in the tides
and tall birds pick in the foliage
for crickets, gnats, or duns,
and the strange cries of the seabirds
drift across the sky
like a memory of paradise, blue,
blue on blue on blue.

. . . so Beatrice took the poet's hand
and began that beauteous ascension
toward the path where Berti
walked in his girdle of leather
clasped in a buckle of bone,
where the cheeks of the women were natural,
without the artificial color,

and kind Mary stayed her hand at the cradle,
smiled upward gently,
and the blue flame of heaven
a thousand miles in her eyes,

and I have seen that light
in the dirt brown eyes of a woman
turning her hand to a craft,
the rhythm of her heart,
o sanguis meus! the exact rhythm
of her blood bound to mine
in the rhythm of our breathing,
and she speaks to me as a light
which opens the gates to wisdom,

and that is *religio*, to re-bind,
that is my religion.

THE JOURNEY HOME

I.
Bright red and orange maple leaves
tumble over clipped lawns
and tidy hedges and roll
down wet concrete gutters;
in the west, a ball of sun sinks
in the sea like a molten silver dollar,
slowly, imperceptibly, sinks in the water.
Down the narrow avenue
the first light of evening falls
pale through the curtains on a window.

II.
In the mountains, rivers move
like silk across the dark
as the sun swims under the earth.
Men and women
no one will ever remember
grope on, dazzled,
blinded by the pitch of night,
seduced by rustling silks
that hang before them like a mirror
reflecting a liquid inner light.

III.
My own footfall
along the deserted road
echoes in the hills: twig-snap,
the muffle of wet leaves.
I've walked this road before.
A pony stamps and snorts,
a dog barks far away.
High overhead, Orion drowns
in a slowly creeping tide
of blue-black cumulus cloud.

IV.
Later, at my cabin,
a small gray moth
trembles in the lamplight.
Soon, the crack of burning wood,
the rich kerosene smell.
The night is so crisp,
so perfectly still,
I can hear beyond the fire
a single alder leaf
fluttering to the ground.

V.
Past midnight I look up
from my book in yellow light.
The pup is curled asleep
on a throw-rug near the stove.
The rocker creaks as I rise.
Outside, the clouds swam silently by
and the Dipper rests in the treetops
and all the heavens shimmer
in trembling protoplasms
of living light.

VI.
I turn the damper down,
blow out the lamp,
and climb the stairs to the loft.
Warm and bare, I stand
looking out of the window.
A soft October breeze
makes silent chimes of all
the luminous, dew-soaked leaves.
Adrift in the starry universe, by the thread
of a single breath, we cling or fall.

VII.

Already the morning mist
gathers in the boughs
of ancient cedars and rolls
across the frost-brushed grasses
on hills above the sea.
One by one, imperceptibly,
the stars begin to fade,
then suddenly all the world
rests at peace in the ivory light,
a living pearl at the break of day.

ISH PROVINCE WORK SONG
after Chuang Tzu

The Plan
is the work.
The work
is play,
joy,

wherein reside
silence
and song
side by side
lighting
the way.

SAPROPHYTE

I have often enough walked
through the thick wet leaves of autumn
to have memorized the deep steps
and rich mulch alive in my nostrils,
have learned somehow in this paucity of decay
that it is here at the dying end of the year
in a rich sump of time
that life, like memory begins,
the first roots creep forth
tiny gray beneath damp earth.
No moon nor stars rise up
among bare limbs and cumulus,
no metaphor survives dull enough
for this dark weather.

Down the valley through dense brush
two coyotes in a thicket
mourn no moon. Nighthawks
dip for moths. Mountain beaver
burrow deeper under heaped slash.
Hoe and axe lie idle in the barn.
An old coon scuttles before me
down the hill through thick salal
and through the cedar saplings.
Mushrooms. Saprophytes. The years
grind on, going nowhere. And here
in dead decaying leaves I wait,
ready to be born.

CUNNILINGUS

Hast thou found a nest softer than cunnus
Or hast thou found better rest . . .
—E.P.

Sometimes, just at dusk,
the long fields rise and fall,
hillocks gently rolling
with the rhythm of a woman
sleeping softly as though
beneath a great cotton comforter
which you would name fog.

And drowning in a dark
so thick it seethes
with the certainty of promise,
I put down my nose to the perfume
of tall damp grasses.
And I breathe.

RUNNING FOR DAYLIGHT

for Bill Ransom

Drawn through the night
by the constant cries of horns
that roll from drifting fog
on the brackish foam of the sea,
I rise from restless sleep at 3 a.m. to run,
knowing their song has torn me
again from the nightmarer's fall:
if you dream yourself down far enough
you drown. Bulwarks groan
in the slosh of waves all down
the decaying pier. The sailors
drifting seaward down the ocean floor
grow mythic when the tolling horns,
leviathan, gently roll
across the shoals of sleeping dogfish
near the shore. Erect on the rocky point
the lighthouse, freshly painted, void of light,
is a pale apparition awash
in the running tide. If you listen
long enough, you'll hear
a distant ferry whistle blow,
its wake recoiled in mucky loam
among pilings sagging 'neath the pier.
In Scorpius above the fog,
Antares brightly shines.
From Kah Tai Lagoon a mousy teal
rises on soundless wings into
the first faint glimmer of dawn
as the horns continue to peal.
The air sharpens like a stick.
The wick of night's dark lamp
burns low. And running the beach until

my blue poisoned lungs explode
my mind with the passionate
intensity of their fire, until
the tortured muscles of my legs revolt
against the rising weight of my feet,
my eyes are filled with waxing light
as though with a dazzling, a burning:
no end in sight.

EPISTLE FOR YULE

Christmas eve. Horns moan sad
in the dark, passive waves
continue to lick the feet
of sturdy cliffs, and maples
months ago reflected our faces
and dropped their leaves
in despair. The little lights
along Port Townsend streets
limp in the crippling dark
of the longest night of the year.

"I'm an old man," the old man said,
"I don't want *any*thing any more."

A storm tears itself hollow
on the shards of Olympic peaks.
A few heavy raindrops
splatter through the fir to the roof
as clouds roll down the canyon
like deer. The river Hoh
rows blindly toward the sea.

I slump indoors, smoking,
reading poetry. Green alder
snaps in the fire. No wind
tonight to stir
the rivulets of rain on leaves
of dark winter salal,
and out at sea at solstice
the lost horns lift their voices
in a litany of moans.

PASTORAL
for Tree

I confess the patter of rain
falling softly in the grass outside my window
lifts my heart from my mind's dark clutches
and the world is feminine and wild and I
am her brooding lover. I confess delight
in the rapid darting flight of starlings
pitched against the breeze, swirling high
above the waves and salty loam as though
such flight were more to them than flight,
a song perhaps played silently, enchanting
the cool autumn air. And the heavy
coastal clouds of winter fail to get me down,
turning the dark cedar forests spruce blue
and glistening under the moonlight where
I am happy for a time.

25:XII:76

SUNRISE, COLUMBIA GORGE
after Su Tung-P'o
for Paul Hansen

I.
Ragged granite peaks
turn from blue to red
to orange, climb skyward
where silent mallards
glide. A logging truck
winds along a road.
The river pulses
like an artery
tying the heartland
to the sun-drenched sea.

II.
With sky bleeding blue,
the slow river browns.
Islands float like clouds.
Green conifer hills,
walls of solid stone
form steep riverbanks
filtering morning light.
Far, far upriver,
a freight train rumbles
like the river rolls.

III.
Gone from home again,
I watch the river
wind toward the sea,
remembering peaks
and rivers winding,
half a life of times
wiled in pastel rooms
rented for a night,
recalling flavors
of savory wines
half a life away.

FIRST PSALM

for Gary & Masa

Where there is water,
the birds carry it up
on glistening wings,
and when it spills from their beaks
we shall raise our eyes and name it: rain;

Where there are forests,
our spirit shall inhabit them
as shadows and as creatures
whose very signatures shine
from the marrow of our bones;

Where there are stars at night,
the eyes of living stone
shall reflect the living flame
and open like a secret
in the frosty quiet light;

Where there is charity,
we hold it in our arms
like wheat, its chaff
ground to the bread of hope
by the dancing of our feet;

Where there is wind in the trees,
small birds shall sail in it,
and the grasses shall bend
as we bend with them, listening
closely, learning how to sing.

SECOND PSALM

Quomodo cantabimus canticum Domini in terra aliena?
How shall we sing the Lord's song in an alien land?

He wakened in the gray light
of just-before-dawn, pulled on
the long woolen socks of his trade,
the short trousers, snapped suspenders,
laced the tall boots and drove
past Kah Tai Lagoon into town.

The incredible music of machines
buzzed inside his ears:
bark of D8 Cat, diesel purr,
theme-songs from tv screens,
echoes of the chainsaw roar.

He doesn't remember
the idiot girl with spittle
dripping from her chin
hurling scotchbroom by the fistful
into the slanting drizzle
and early morning wind.

He doesn't remember the heron,
tall on a straw-thin leg
standing motionless and glaring.
He doesn't remember the child laughing
under the slow steady beat
of broad blue wings.

He smokes a slow cigarette
and reads the morning paper
and drinks his coffee black.
He faintly hears, he thinks,
the music of machines.
And all too soon he learns
the terrible truths they sing.

THIRD PSALM

Out of roots grown white and swoll
that sift the earthy depths
of sand, rock, clay: soil;

Out of soil sifting and sorting
crystal drops of water
fallen from the sky;

Out of blue sky and gray,
stars blazing night and day,
the sun's warm *shine*;

Out of the sun-warm leafy tips
of lofty branches
on ancient aging trees;

Out of roots and branches,
out of sunlight and moonlight and rain,
out of grasses, brushes and trees

come all the air we breathe.

FOURTH PSALM
for Sam Green

South of narrow cirrus clouds
a few stars softly pulse
in the night's dark blue.
Half a moon wears the clouds
like a fine lace veil. Light fog
lingers among bare alder boughs.

Wanting to make you a song,
I walked an old logging road
salal has half reclaimed, and
found song in the names of things:
cattail, camas, and thistle,
kinikinick, and yew.

I cannot make you a poem to sing
the fragrance of scotchbroom
blooming in the night. The song
sings itself in the heart of things,
the poem is in the chimney-smoke
vanishing in the clear, still air.

21:III:78
for Tree

It is the first day of spring
and the tiny hard alderbuds
have burst overnight
into small green miniatures of leaves.
East of the reds and blues of sunset,
the moon, nearly full,
blooms. Soon, the nighthawks
will return in a flurry of wings
and strange reptillian cries.

The dog drags home the gnawed
half-picked carcass
of a chicken, the cavity squeaky clean
as a motel sink, and hangs it
on the porch like a dead angel.
For over an hour
the small bones pop between his jaws,
the fleshy gristle ground
to a fine meaty flour.

As shadows climb through the sky,
a flock of nuthatches rises
from the small bare limbs
and vanishes in a stand of fir.
Six years this season, we've worked
side by side. Finally, we begin.
Out there it is equinox, everything
in balance, everything living
and dying. Every thing all right.

GETTING THE RHYTHM RIGHT

Lousewort,
maidenhair,
dogwood and salal:
'round and around,
the turbulence of what grows
everywhere,

wild (as the heart is
and no wonder
there is such fear,
the awesome natural beauty
of the wild (as the heart is
uncivilized
and chaotic however balanced
(*chung*: centered)
in its struggle

the long fingers of roots
dip down into the earth
smelling rich
as sour sweat
or the thick human odor
of laundry day
or of what's described
as fishy
(how we multiply!)

groping down into the dark
into wet recesses
reaching there
whatever is moist, is damp
which brings us to flower
and through,

to fruition—

the raspberry's red,
the blackberry's blue,
the blue Olympic Range
looming through the rain,
the rain,
the great upward-reaching limbs
of ancient trees
with mosses
like pubic hair
thick in their crotches,

and the wind is a tumult,
the many breaths of the wind
curling back
and mixing, inter-
twining
(as we do)
sometimes confused, swirling
in that ecstatic gasping,

rain,
milk of the breast
of sky,
sky blue-gray or blue-blue,

and at the breast of a woman
I lay in half-sleep,
the mind rich with lousewort
smelling muscadine,
tangle of dogwood
flowering at my heart,
and asked in a dream,

"what is it
in a man
retains the common dignity
of the feminine,
the mothering instinct
and regenerative intuition,
and how out of turbulence
and tumult
the saprophytic affections grow"

and traced there on her back
the long deep river of her spine
until it fell
into hillocks or into mind,

and memory settles into sediment,
the conscious mind demurs,
the rain tattoos the roof
and I match my breathing to hers.

ECSTATIC DRUNK, OLD-FASHIONED SONG COMING FORWARD

for Olga

Let me sing
of the male and female in my heart,
let me sing of the opulence of stars,
male and female in the soul;
let me coil like a horned dragon,
wait like an insect,
then salamander a slither;
let me sing up the heron and the wren
in a song of eternal beginning;
let me sing horsehair and feather,
charms, chants, and bedazzling,
of the breasts of forgiving mothers
and of the gentleness of fathers;

"Unity & Morality are secondary considerations,
& belong to Philosophy & not
to Poetry, to Exception
& not to Rule, to Accident
& not to Substance; the Ancients call'd it
eating of the tree of Good & Evil."
—thus, Blake, on the classic;

and let me sing then of Blake
and of Whitman,
forebears,
of old Ezra the Idaho Kid,
poor Emily alone in all her rooms;

let me conjure a masculine
as well as a feminine muse,

worshipping man and woman
singly and altogether,
that communion is holy;

may my little songs raze/
raise the conscience of the guilty
and elate, elating
exculpate
immaculate innocent visions;

may my songs carry the odor of the nether—
groin, pubis, penis, mons veneris—
the gates of heaven
through which
the azure first is grasped, first glimpsed
and then grasped,
oh the caress!
the caressing grip of the mind!

let me sing
my sisters and my brothers from their chains—

I am a poet, gentle,
and give this poem
authority to caress;
I am a father and gentle
and inform this poem
with forgiveness—may my hand
be the hand of a never-jealous lover
and alien to the glove;

I am congenitally male,
proud to be gentle,
and pray this poem a power

of love that lasts forever;
and I am human to the end,
male and female,
ecstatic in that struggle,
and I pray for a healing song;

I am a poet, gentle,
and pray for the golden phoenix
to rise from the wasted ash
of the tattered human soul;

I am a man of peace,
loving both men and women,
who loves without shame
the bird, the beast, and the flower,
and for these,
ecstatic also together,
I sing this archaic prayer:

singly,
under the scoop of the Dipper
drifting northward through the evening
our songs grow feeble;
in this song
we join our hands as the People,
and together,
in love and healing,
together singing,
we relearn the ancient power.

photo: Fred Willard

SAM HAMILL was born in 1942 and grew up in Utah. He is the author of the following books of poems: *Heroes of the Teton Mythos*, *Uintah Blue* (a chapbook), *Petroglyphs*, *The Calling Across Forever*, *Living Light* (a chapbook), *Triada*; he also is author of a collection of essays, *At Home in the World*. He works as co-publisher of Copper Canyon Press and homesteads with Tree Swenson in the Ish Province of the Oregonian Biome.

This book was designed by Tree Swenson and Sam Hamill. The type is Bembo, a copy of a roman cut by Francesco Griffo for the Venetian printer Aldus Manutius. It was first used in Cardinal Bembo's *De Aetna* in 1495. The illustrations are by Tree Swenson and are based on petroglyphs located in Ish Province.